Thank God

PRAYERS OF JEWS AND CHRISTIANS TOGETHER

Carol Frances Jegen, BVM

Rabbi Byron L. Sherwin

Liturgy Training Publications

Liturgy Training Publications
1800 North Hermitage Avenue
Chicago IL 60622-1101
1-800-933-1800

Art by Joan Goldin. Design by Ana Stephenson.
Printed in the United States of America.

ISBN 0-929650-05-0

CONTENTS

FOREWORD

The compilers of these texts have looked to Jewish and Christian traditions for prayers, commentaries and reflections that are filled with or are about thanksgiving. These have been organized according to moments and images. For each such unit, a principal text has been chosen. It is followed by a variety of other texts.

Except for those texts from the Hebrew Scriptures or the Christian New Testament, sources are not given with the texts themselves but have been placed on the final pages of this collection. They are arranged by unit and by the first words of each text.

The criteria for including passages in this book had to do with the strength and beauty of a text, but also with a particular suitability. The compilers sought words that could be used by both Jews and Christians and, especially, those that could be used by Jews and Christians together. We have in common the biblical roots of our prayers, especially the psalms. But there is more. We have not often shared other compositions, but sometimes that sharing is possible and authentic. There are times when we need to speak words in common.

This book is intended for times when Jews and Christians gather, whether in small groups where neighborhood provides a bond or in study groups from churches and synagogues or in larger assemblies for interfaith services of prayer. For any of these, let this book serve as a resource. A simple order of prayer is provided following the texts; this can be adapted as needed. Because Thanksgiving Day has become a day for interfaith prayer in many communities in the United States, an order of service for that day has also been included.

This book is the work of Byron L. Sherwin, a rabbi and professor at Spertus College of Judaica in Chicago, and Carol Frances Jegen, a Sister of Charity of the Blessed Virgin Mary and a professor at Mundelein College in Chicago. Each has long worked within the Jewish-Christian dialogue both in academic and congregational settings. The authors and the publisher will appreciate your insights into the task undertaken in these pages and your reflections and contributions to further collections of texts that can be shared by Jews and Christians.

Gabe Huck

INTRODUCTION

*A*n elder once said to a child, "I will give you a gold coin if you can tell me where God dwells."

"I will give you two if you can tell me where God does not dwell," answered the child.

"How expansive are your works, O Lord! The world is full of your works." (Psalm 104:24) Each particle of creation bears testimony to the presence of God. Each soul of each cell bears a message from the creator and sustainer of all. A divine invitation is addressed to each of us.

The surprise of being alive, of awakening to a renewed gift of life, evokes our wonder. Witnessing the marvels of creation overcomes us with awe. Discovering that what we readily take for granted is the miraculous in disguise overwhelms us with humility. Gratitude is awe and wonder. Everyday awe and wonder is our response to God's grace. In receiving a blessing, we return a prayer. Humility is the prelude to thanksgiving. Awareness of the source of all blessings evokes our blessing.

It would be ungracious not to be grateful. "How can I repay unto the Lord all God's bountiful dealings with me?" (Psalm 116:12) What we own, we owe. "The earth is the Lord's." (Psalm 24:1) We are trustees, stewards of a treasure entrusted to our care. Not to use the treasure as the owner intends would be negligence. In thanksgiving we join the choir of creation.

Thanksgiving is bearing witness that no one is "self-made." Each of us emerges into life from God's love. Each breath is a gift of God. Our daily bread is the product of the divine largess. The daily sunrise is a reminder that creation is a perpetual gift. When we seem to burst with love, it is an echo of God's love for us.

We are commanded not to make an image of God (Exodus 20:4), yet God made such an image by creating us (Genesis 1:27). God is reflected in each human soul. Friendship and family are pathways to perceiving God's presence in the most intimate of human relations. Those whom we cherish are emissaries from one who cherishes us all.

With notes given by God we each compose a tune, a life. We return a song to God. Appreciation becomes the vehicle of celebration. We offer thanksgiving for what we have received in order that we may then thank God even for the ability to give.

Do we sometimes remain void of gratitude? Then a proverb advises us: "If you cannot be thankful for what you have received, be thankful for what you have been spared." Or, a second proverb can be evoked: "Rather than have what we want, we should want what we have."

We offer these prayers and other texts to those who join creation's choir. The texts are like strings linking the giver and the recipient. In their recitation, the two are brought closer.

Once a child was flying a kite so high it could not be seen. "How do you know it is still there?" asked an adult. "Because," responded the child, "I feel the tug from above."

That is the intent of all that follows here. As Jews and as Christians we have this to say alone and together, "Thank God!"

Byron L. Sherwin
Carol Frances Jegen
October 3, 1989
Two hundredth anniversary of George
    Washington's Thanksgiving Proclamation

I will give thanks to you, O LORD,
with all my heart . . .
in the presence of the angels I will sing your praise.

Psalm 138:1

Now thank we all our God
With hearts and hands and voices,
Who wondrous things has done,
In whom this world rejoices,
Who from our mothers' arms
Has blessed us on our way
With countless gifts of love
And still is ours today.

I am commanded—therefore, I am. There is a built-in sense of indebtedness in the consciousness of man, an awareness of owing gratitude, of being called upon at certain moments to reciprocate, to answer, to live in a way which is compatible with the grandeur and mystery of living.

Rejoice always. Pray without ceasing. In all circumstances give thanks.
First Letter to the Thessalonians 5:16–18

As I give myself to the task of writing the story
Of years now gone by; of describing the course of events
Lived through the days of time past until now;
I come to the end of a life whose term is uncertain.
I pray you, omnipotent God, in your care for me, help me.
If this work finds favor with you, inspire me, favor me.
Grant that this writing, my offspring, be born;
Grant that my wish be fulfilled so that, thanks to your help
I may recount all your blessings.
To you do I owe every moment of life, from the first,
When I breathed in the luminous air of existence.
Protected by you, I have passed through the tempests and storms
Of the world, hostile and fickle.
The twelfth week of my years has already passed;
Since then, I have counted six burning seasons of sun,
Summer's heat; as many of ice-frozen winters.
These are your gift to me, O my God. You renew
The cycle of years which have passed; you bring back
The course of time, making it retread the path once taken.
May I, then, be granted the time and the favor
To celebrate all your goodness, to sing your gracious deeds,
In a poem whose language bears witness to all that I feel

Of thanksgiving to you.
This thanks, though concealed in our heart,
Is already known to you. I do not doubt this;
But my voice, aware of the secret, would snatch it out
From the silent depths of my soul and let flow the course
Of my hopes and desires, which now pour forth in abundance.

The time for reciting the morning prayers almost had past and still the Rabbi of Apt had not yet appeared at the synagogue. His disciples sought him out, and found him in his study, smoking his pipe, lost in thought.

"Master, the time for reciting the morning prayers is almost past," they said, breaking his intense concentration.

"I know," he said, "Early this morning, I arose and I began to recite the prayer 'I offer thanks to you . . .' and since then I have been thinking one thought: Who am *I* that I deign to offer thanks to you?"

Let us give thanks to the Lord our God.
It is right to give God thanks and praise.

We give you thanks, O God,
  we give thanks,
and we invoke your name;
    we declare your wondrous deeds.

Psalm 75:2

Praised are you, Lord our God, ruler of the universe,
who has placed such beauty as this in the world.

Praised are you, Lord our God, ruler of the universe,
who graciously bestows favor upon the undeserving,
even as you have bestowed favor upon me.
    May God who has been gracious to you
    continue to favor you with all that is good.

Every day
When prayers rise
In synagogue, church and mosque,
God prays for his world:
May it be the will of my children
To accept my gift of life,
And allow me to lead them
Toward the light.

Glory be to God for dappled things—
    For skies of couple-color as a brindled cow;
      For rose-moles all in stipple upon trout that swim;
Fresh-firecoal chestnut-falls; finches' wings;
    Landscape plotted and pieced—fold, fallow, and plough;
      And all trades, their gear and tackle and trim.

All things counter, original, spare, strange;
    Whatever is fickle, freckled (who knows how?)
      With swift, slow; sweet, soul; adazzle, dim;
He fathers-forth whose beauty is past change:
                Praise him.

There is a question which follows me wherever I turn. What is expected of me? What is demanded of me? . . . With every child born a new expectation enters the world. . . . Indebtedness is given with our very being. It is not derived from conceptions; it lives in us as an awareness before it is conceptualized or clarified in content. It means having a task, being called. It experiences living as receiving, not only as taking. Its content is gratitude for a gift received. Indebtedness is the pathos of being human, self-awareness of the self as committed; it is given with the awareness of existence.

All you who worship him, bless the God of gods, praise him and give him thanks, for his love is everlasting. *Daniel 3:90*

 We praise you, Lord
 for our rooted feet:
 by the thousand
 with sycamore and pine, we stand
 deep in your soil. We grow
 in halos of light
 and in a world where nothing signals
 but in barks and grunts and cries
 we scratch our signs on papyrus and steel
 and with gladness of mind and tongue
  say your name.

To be a person is to reciprocate. Reciprocity involves appreciation. Biologically we all take in and give off. I become a person by knowing the meaning of receiving and giving. I become a person when I begin to reciprocate.

It is good to give thanks to the LORD,
   to sing praise to your name, Most High,
To proclaim your kindness at dawn
     and your faithfulness throughout the night,
With ten-stringed instrument and lyre,
     with melody upon the harp.
For you make me glad, O LORD, by your deeds;
     at the works of your hands I rejoice.
How great are your works, O LORD!
     How very deep are your thoughts!

Psalm 92:1–6

Praised are you, Lord our God, ruler of the universe,
who creates fruit of the ground.

We give thanks to you for every drop you have caused to fall for us. Praise to you,
God, to whom abundant thanksgiving is due.

As clay are we, as soft and yielding clay
That lies between the fingers of the potter.
At his will he molds it thick or thin,
And forms its shape according to his fancy.
So are we in your hand, God of love:
	Recall your covenant and show your mercy.

As stone are we, inert, resistless stone
That lies within the fingers of the mason.
At his will he keeps it firm and whole,
Or at his pleasure hews it into fragments.
So are we in your hand, God of life:
	Recall your covenant and show your mercy.

Praised are you, Lord our God, ruler of the universe,
who have withheld nothing from your world
and have created beautiful creatures and beautiful trees for mortals to enjoy.

Most high, almighty, good Lord God, to you belong praise, glory, honor and all blessing.

Praised be my Lord God, with all your creatures, and especially our brother the sun, who brings us the day and who brings us the light: fair is he, and he shines with a very great splendor. O Lord, he signifies you to us.

Praised be my Lord for our sister the moon, and for the stars, which you have set clear and lovely in the heaven.

Praised be my Lord for our brother the wind, and for air and clouds, calms and all weather, by which you uphold life and all creatures.

Praised be my Lord for our sister water, who is very serviceable to us, and humble and precious and clean.

Praised be my Lord for our brother fire, through whom you give us light in the darkness; he is bright and pleasant and mighty and strong.

Praised be my Lord for our mother the earth, which sustains and keeps us and brings forth all kinds of fruits and flowers of many colors and the grass.

Praised be my Lord for all those who pardon one another for love's sake, and who endure weakness and tribulation. Blessed are they who peacefully shall endure, for you, O Most High, will give them a crown.

Praised be my Lord for our sister, the death of the body, from which no one escapes. Blessed are those who die in your most holy will.

Praise and bless the Lord and give thanks to God and serve God with great humility.

Father, all-powerful
	and ever-living God,
we do well always and everywhere
	to give you thanks.
All things are of your making,
all times and seasons obey your laws,
but you chose to create us in your own image,
setting us over the whole world in all its wonder.
You made us the steward of creation,
to praise you day by day for the marvels
	of your wisdom and power.

Earth's crammed with heaven
And every common bush
    afire with God.
But only he who sees,
takes off his shoes.

We are as you have made us—
we belong heart and soul to this earth.
Keep us in this grace,
make us faithful to your creation
and teach us to recognize,
in gratitude and delight,
that everything that you have done
is good.

Blessed are you, O God,
Creator of the universe,
who have made all things good
and given the earth for us to cultivate.
Grant that we may always use created things gratefully
and share your gifts with those in need.

Almighty and ever-living God,
you have made us stewards over the created world,
so that in all things we might honor the demands of charity.
Graciously hear our prayers,
that your blessing may come upon all those
who use these objects for their needs.
Let them always see you as the good surpassing every good
and love their neighbor with upright hearts.

When the Holy One, praised be he, created the first human couple, he took them and led them around the trees of the Garden of Eden and said to them: "Behold my works, how beautiful and commendable they are. All that I have created, I have created for you. Be careful not to corrupt or destroy my world! For if you corrupt it, there will be no one after you to repair it."

For the fruit of all creation, thanks be to God.
For his gifts to every nation, thanks be to God.
For the plowing, sowing, reaping,
    silent growth while we are sleeping,
    future needs in earth's safe-keeping, thanks be to God.

For the just reward of labor, God's will be done.
In the help we give our neighbor, God's will be done.
In our worldwide task of caring
    for the hungry and despairing,
    in the harvest we are sharing, God's will be done.

For the harvests of the spirit, thanks be to God.
For the good we all inherit, thanks be to God.
For the wonders that astound us,
    for the truths that still confound us
    most of all that love has found us, thanks be to God.

The sun to rule in the day,
  for God's great love is without end;
The moon and the stars in the night,
  for God's great love is without end.

Psalm 136:8–9

You illumine the world and its creatures with mercy; in your goodness, day after day you renew creation. How manifold your works, O Lord; with wisdom you fashioned them all. The earth abounds with your creations. Uniquely exalted since earliest time, enthroned on praise and prominence since the world began, eternal God, with your manifold mercies continue to love us, our pillar of strength, protecting rock, sheltering shield, sustaining stronghold.

Praised are you, Lord our God, ruler of the universe whose word brings the evening dusk. You open the gates of dawn with wisdom, change the day's divisions with understanding, set the succession of seasons, and arrange the stars in the sky according to your will. You create day and night, rolling light away from darkness and darkness away from light. Eternal God, your rule shall embrace us forever. Praised are you, Lord, for each evening's dusk.

O God, who made the sun, you are the sun of my soul and I love your radiance. I love you, O light eternal; grant that I may see you in the brightness of your glory.

O God, whose hand has spread the sky
And all its shining hosts on high,
And painting it with fiery light
Made it so beauteous and so bright:

Thus when the fourth day was begun,
You made the circle of the sun,
And set the moon for ordered change
And planets for their wider range.

My Father, Father of orphans,
be gracious unto me,
send me the sun's rays as a gift.
And I, an orphan of orphans,
shall receive your gift with thanks, with love, with hope.
I know how to prize your gift, your goodness.
My heart sings and shouts to you,
O Father of life,
blessed are you.

I give thanks to you, O Lord, for you have illumined my face with the light of your covenant. Day by day I seek you and ever you shine upon me, bright as the perfect dawn.

O King of glory, I ask of you as an alms
to admit me to the house of hospitality,
where I will seek neither food nor raiment,
but be for ever gazing on and listening to the glory.

We should thank and praise, laud and glorify, exalt and honor, extol and adore God who performed all these miracles for our ancestors and for us. God brought us from slavery to freedom, from sorrow to joy, from mourning to festivity, from darkness to great light, and from bondage to redemption. Let us then sing unto God a new song: Halleluya, praise the Lord!

O Lord our God,
make us lie down in peace,
and raise us up, O our king, to life.

To you I pray, O LORD;
at dawn you hear my voice;
at dawn I bring my plea expectantly before you.

Psalm 5:3–4

Who was ever so wake
as this wakening day?
Not just brooklet and brake,
but the roof, too, is gay,

with its tiles that outstand
in the blue of the sky,
as alive as a land
and as full of reply.

Breathing thanks are conveyed.
All nocturnal affliction
had vanished with night,

whose darkness was made
—O pure contradiction!—
from legions of light.

I am grateful to you, living, enduring ruler, for restoring my soul to me in compassion. You are faithful beyond measure.

Praised are you, Lord our God, ruler of the universe,
for granting us life, for sustaining us,
and for causing us to reach this day.

When they sang together, when my morning stars sang as the night was ending and light came up from all sides; when the night was ending, the darkness expelled, and my sun rose in the east; when my thoughts shook off slumber and my limbs woke from their sleep of night—then I sought to greet the dawn with music and to worship with song.

In the morning let me know your love
for I put my trust in you.
Make me know the way I should walk;
to you I lift up my soul.

Psalm 143:8

Of the light of dawn let none be silent,
Nor let the bright stars be wanting in praise;
Let all the fountains of the rivers lift up their songs. . . .
So let all powers on earth cry aloud: Amen, Amen.
Might and honor, glory and praise to God,
Only giver of all that is good. Amen. Amen.

As soon as I lie down, I fall peacefully asleep,
for you alone, O LORD,
bring security to my dwelling.

Psalm 4:9

I give thanks to you, O Lord, for your eye is ever awake, watching over my soul.

Have mercy on me, Lord, and bring me free from the darkness and the shadow of
death. Call me into your glorious light. Lighten my darkness, O splendor of eternal
light, O day that has no evening.

Praised are you, Lord our God, ruler of the universe who with wisdom fashioned the human body, creating openings, arteries, glands and organs, marvelous in structure, intricate in design. Should but one of them, by being blocked or opened, fail to function, it would be impossible to exist. Praised are you, Lord, healer of all flesh who sustains our bodies in wondrous ways.

We are the work of your hands, O God.
You, Lord, have made us and love us.
All our life is your gift,
all your power was in
our creation
and thus you will go on giving to us
grace upon grace.
What more need we hope for
from you?
This certainty—God—
is good enough for us.

We give you thanks,
God our Father,
For having created us
Each different from the other.
Our faces radiate every color
And your light plays over their variety.
We thank you for having given us
A variety of languages,
Thus varying our quest for you
In human forms of expression.

Before I was born your love enveloped me.
You turned nothing into substance, and created me.
Who etched out my frame? Who poured
Me into a vessel and molded me?
Who breathed a spirit into me? Who opened
The womb of Sheol and extracted me?
Who has guided me from youth-time until now?
Taught me knowledge, and cared wondrously for me?
Truly, I am nothing but clay within your hand.
It is you, not I, who have really fashioned me.
I confess my sin to you, and do not say
That a serpent intrigued, and tempted me.
How can I conceal from you my faults, since
Before I was born your love enveloped me?

For every breath one takes, one must offer praise to the Holy One, praised be he.

With open ears,
    we take in the joy of music,
    the delight of poetry,
    and the simple songs of daily life.
For all of these blessings, we are filled with gratitude.
We are also thankful
    for those persons who teach us how to listen:
    for poets, musicians,
    parents, prophets and teachers.
Grateful are we for that long line of holy people
    from the East and the West
    who teach us to listen
    for the echo of your divine voice
    in all words of truth.
Praised are you, Lord our God,
    for the gift of hearing.

When one dresses, one should say: "Praise to God who clothes the naked."

The eyes of all hope in you, LORD,
  And you give them food in due season.
You open your hand,
  And every creature is filled with your blessings.

Psalm 104:27–28

Lord, bless this food we are about to eat. May it do us good in body and soul. If there are any poor creatures walking the road in hunger and thirst, may God bring them in to us so that we may share this food with them as God shared good things with us.

From many homes and of many ages
we stand at this common table, Lord,
and we give you thanks.
For you have been the story our ancestors told
to their children and their children's children
until that story came to us.
You are the story we tell
in all our various ways
to the coming generation.
We remember now those who have died.
We thank you, Lord, for the delight we find
in one another and in the good things of your earth.
Bless us and keep us.
Make your face shine on us and be kind to us.
Turn your face toward us and give us peace.

Praise to you, Lord, God of all creation,
for you feed the whole world with your goodness
with grace, with loving kindness and tender mercy.
You give food to all creatures,
and your loving kindness endures forever.
Because of your great goodness
food has never failed us;
O may it not fail us for ever and ever
for the sake of your great name.
You nourish and sustain all creatures
and do good to all.
Praise to you, O Lord, for you give food to all.

Praised are you, Lord our God, ruler of the universe,
who brings forth bread from the earth.

Praised are you, Lord our God, ruler of the universe,
who creates various kinds of nourishment.

Praised are you, Lord our God, ruler of the universe,
who creates the fruit of the vine.

Earthmaker and Lord of all creation,
    we are mindful that this food before us
    has already been blessed by sun, earth and rain.
We pause to be grateful
    for the hidden gifts of life in this food.
Bless our eyes and taste
    so that we may eat this food
    in a holy and mindful manner.
We lift up this bread
    may it be food and symbol
    for all of us who shall eat it.

The hasidic master Rabbi Barukh of Medziboz reflected on the sentence in the Grace
after Meals: "For all of this, O Lord, we thank you," and he translated the sentence as,
"For all this, we thank you for being our Lord."

I will praise the name of God with a song,
I will magnify God with thanksgiving.

Psalm 69:31–32

With saintly shout, and solemn jubilee,
Where the bright seraphim in burning row
Their loud up-lifted angel-trumpets blow,
And the cherubic host in thousand choirs
Touch their immortal harps of golden wires,
With those just spirits that wear victorious palms,
Hymns devout and holy psalms
Singing everlastingly;
That we on earth with undiscording voice
May rightly answer that melodious noise;
As once we did, till disproportion'd sin
Jarr'd against Nature's chime, and with harsh din
Broke the fair music that all creatures made
To their great Lord, whose love their motion sway'd
In perfect diapason, whilst they stood
In first obedience, and their state of good.

In receiving a pleasure, we must return a prayer; in attaining a success, we radiate compassion. We have the right to consume because we have the power to celebrate.

All your works shall praise you, O Lord our God, and your pious ones, the just who do your will, together with all your people, the house of Israel, shall praise you in joyous song. They shall thank, exalt, revere and sanctify you, and ascribe sovereignty to your name, O our King. For it is good to give thanks to you, and it is fitting to sing praises to your name, for you are God from everlasting to everlasting.

Lord, may the seeds of the tree of stillness bear fruit
    for us and for all the restless world.
Praised are you, Lord our God,
    who gives to us nourishment
    in times of silence and solitude.

The psalm, "For singing to our God is good," can be interpreted to mean: "It is good if we can bring about that God sings within us."

Once, on the eve of the Day of Atonement, Rabbi Zusya heard a cantor in the House of Prayer, chanting the words: "And it is forgiven," in strange and beautiful tones. Then he called to God: "Lord of the world! Had Israel not sinned, how could such a song have been intoned before you?"

Through song man climbs to the highest palace. From that palace he can influence the universe and its prisons. Song is Jacob's ladder forgotten on earth by the angels. Sing and you shall defeat death; sing and you shall disarm the foe.

Singing is discovered and invented. It is born at times when there is no other possible way for people to express themselves—at the grave, for example, where four or five people with untrained, clumsy voices sing words that are greater and smaller than their faith and their experience.

The marvels of God are not brought forth from one's self. Rather, it is more like a chord, a sound that is played. The tone does not come out of the chord itself, but rather, through the touch of the musician. I am, of course, the lyre and harp of God's kindness.

We give thanks to God always for all of you, remembering you in our prayers. What thanksgiving, then, can we render to God for you, for all the joy we feel on your account before our God? May the Lord make you increase and abound in love for one another and for all, just as we have for you, so as to strengthen your hearts, to be blameless in holiness.

First Letter to the Thessalonians 1:2, 3:9, 12–13

Once there was a man named Honi. In times of drought, he would draw a circle around himself and entreat God to make rain fall. Since he always was successful at this task, he acquired the name "the Circle-Drawer."

Honi the Circle-Drawer was troubled by the meaning of a verse in the Psalms (126:1): "When the Lord brought back those who returned to Zion, we were like unto them that dream." Honi knew that the Babylonian exile referred to in this verse had lasted 70 years. "How is it possible," he asked himself, "that someone should sleep for 70 years without interruption?"

One day, while walking on the road, Honi noticed an old man planting a carob tree. Said Honi to the man, "You know it takes 70 years before a carob tree bears fruit. Can you assume you will live 70 years to be able to eat the fruit of this tree?"

"I found this world provided with carob trees," the man replied. "As my ancestors planted for me, so I plant for those who will come after me."

Honi then sat down to eat and he was overcome by sleep. As he slept, a grotto was formed around him, so that he was screened off from sight. He slept for 70 years. When he awoke, he saw a man gathering carobs from the carob tree and eating them.

"Do you know who planted this carob tree?" Honi asked.

"My grandfather," the man replied.

"I must have slept for 70 years!" Honi exclaimed.

Honi then went to his house and asked whether the son of Honi the Circle-Drawer was still alive. He was told that his son had died long ago, but that his grandson was living in the town.

"I *am* Honi," he said. But no one believed him.

Honi then went to the House of Study. There he heard the scholars say, "Our studies are as clear to us today as they were in the times of Honi the Circle-Drawer, for when he came to the House of Study, he would explain all the difficulties in the texts that perplexed the sages."

Honi listened for a while, and he said, "But I *am* Honi the Circle-Drawer." No one would believe him or show him the respect due him.

Honi searched to see if any of his friends were still alive, but he learned that all of them were dead. All of this grieved him deeply, and he prayed to God that he might die. And he died. When this became known, a proverb was coined, "Either friendship or death." Without friendship and companionship, life could hardly be worth living.

Almighty Father,
you are lavish in bestowing all your gifts,
and we give you thanks for the favors you have given us.
In your goodness you have favored us
and kept us safe in the past.
We ask that you continue to protect us
and to shelter us in the shadow of your wings.

We are your people, and you are our God.
We are your children, and you our father.
We are your servants, and you our master.
We are your congregation, and you our portion.
We are your inheritance, and you our lot.
We are your flock, and you our shepherd.
We are your vineyard, and you our keeper.
We are your work, and you our creator.
We are your faithful, and you our beloved.
We are your loyal ones, and you our Lord.
We are your devoted people, and you our exalted God.

From Egypt you redeemed us, from the house of bondage you delivered us. In famine you nourished us, in prosperity you sustained us. You rescued us from the sword, protected us from pestilence, and saved us from severe and lingering disease. To this day your compassion has helped us, your kindness has not forsaken us. Never abandon us, Lord our God. These limbs which you formed for us, this soul-force which you breathed into us, this tongue which you set in our mouth, must laud, praise, extol, exalt, and sing your holiness and sovereignty.

My soul proclaims the greatness of the Lord,
my spirit rejoices in God my Savior,
for you, Lord, have looked with favor on your lowly servant.
You have shown strength with your arm
and scattered the proud in their conceit,

casting down the mighty from their thrones
and lifting up the lowly
You have filled the hungry with good things
and sent the rich away empty.
You have come to the aid of your servant Israel,
to remember the promise of mercy,
the promise made to our forebears,
to Abraham and his children for ever.

Luke 1:46–48, 51–55

Worship the Lord in gladness, come before him with joy.
    Enter his gates with thanksgiving,
    with gratitude sing out his praise.
The Lord, creator of the heavens and the earth,
provides food for the hungry with mercy.
The Lord brings justice to the oppressed.
    Praise the creator who works great wonders,
    who ennobles us from birth, who treats us with compassion.
How shall we thank God for our blessings?
    Let us share our bread with the hungry;
    let us not turn away from the needy.
Clothe the naked and shelter the homeless,
help those who have no help.
    Sing a new song for the Lord.
    Where the faithful gather, let God be praised.

May you always bear witness to the love of God in this world
so that the afflicted and the needy
will find in you generous friends,
and welcome you into the joys of heaven.

O my God,
give me strength never to disown the poor,
never before insolent might to bow the head.
Give me strength to raise my spirit high above daily trifles,
lightly to bear my joys and sorrows
and in love to surrender all my strength to your will
for great are your gifts to me.

Lord God,
by the mouth of your prophet Amos you tell us:
"I hate and despise your feasts,
I want none of your burnt offerings.
Let me have no more of the din of your chanting,
no more of your strumming on harps.
But let justice flow like water,
and integrity like an unfailing stream."
Let our feasts
be to come to the aid of the poor and the oppressed,
our song be to practice justice,
and our sacrifice be the offering of a contrite and humble heart.
Then, when our lips sing to you,
our hearts will be celebrating a feast
and you will love our song.

You changed my mourning into dancing;
you took off my sackcloth
and clothed me with gladness,
That my soul might sing praise to you
without ceasing;
O LORD, my God, forever will I give you thanks.

Psalm 30:12–13

Praise to the All-merciful who has given you back to us
and has not given you to the dust.

There are four [classes of people] who have to offer thanksgiving: those who have
crossed the sea, those who have transversed the wilderness, one who has recovered
from an illness, and a prisoner who has been set free. . . . What blessing should the
[freed prisoner] say: Praised be God who bestows loving kindness.

Late have I loved you,
O beauty so ancient and so new;
Late have I loved you!
For behold you were within me,
And I outside;
And I sought you outside
And in my unloveliness
Fell upon those lovely things
That you have made.
    You were with me
And I was not in you.

I was kept from you by those things,
Yet had they not been in you
They would not have been at all.
      You did call and cry to me
And break open my deafness;
And you sent forth your beams
to shine upon me
and chase away my blindness.
You breathed fragrance upon me,
and I drew in my breath
and do now pant for you;
I tasted you
and now hunger and thirst for you.
You touched me,
and I burned for your peace.

How thankful we should be to God
For many deeds of kindness to us!
      Had God freed us from the Egyptians,
      And not sustained us in the wilderness for forty years,
      Dayenu, it would have been sufficient!

Had God sustained us in the wilderness for forty years,
And not fed us with manna,
Dayenu!
    Had God fed us with manna,
    And not given us the Sabbath,
      Dayenu!
Had God given us the Sabbath,
And not brought us to Mount Sinai,
Dayenu!
    Had God brought us to Mount Sinai,
    And not given us the Torah,
      Dayenu!

Let your mercy be upon us, as our hope is in you. Help us, Lord our God, and deliver us. Gather us, and free us from oppression, that we may praise your glory, that we may be exalted in praising you. All the nations you have created, Lord, will worship you and glorify you. Great are you, wondrous are your deeds; you alone are God. We are your people, the flock you shepherd. We will never cease thanking you, recounting your praises to all generations.

MODELS FOR AN ORDER OF SERVICE

I. A Gathering of Jews and Christians

A. A Short Service

CALL TO WORSHIP

Come, bless the LORD,
All you servants of the LORD.
—PSALM 134:1

READING

The reading is from scripture or from another appropriate source. The texts in this collection may be helpful in making this selection. Some moments of silent reflection may follow the reading. One or more persons may then wish to share a reflection on the reading.

PSALM

If the group meets frequently, it may be possible for all to know the words to Psalm 117 by heart.

Praise the Lord, all nations;
 All peoples, glorify God,
Whose grace, like a wave, surges over us,
 Whose faithfulness lasts for all time.
  Praise the Lord!

PRAYER

Those participating may be invited to speak their own prayers, or prayers from this collection may be selected beforehand.

VERSE

May the Lord protect us, coming and going,
now and for ever. Amen.

B. A Longer Service

The same order is observed: call to worship; readings (each followed by silent reflection and shared response); a psalm (prayed with one group alternating with the other); prayers and a closing verse. See the Thanksgiving Day Service below as a model. One or more hymns in which all can take part are appropriate: one near the beginning, one at the conclusion. This collection should be used as a resource in finding texts appropriate to various occasions for gathering.

II. Thanksgiving Day

Come, let us sing to the LORD;
    Let us shout to our saving rock!

Enter God's presence with praise,
    With music and shouts of joy.
—PSALM 95:1–2

HYMN

One of the following or another hymn may be sung.

Now thank we all our God
With hearts and hands and voices,
Who wondrous things has done,
In whom this world rejoices;
Who, from our mothers' arms,
Hath blessed us on our way
With countless gifts of love,
And still is ours today.

— ■ —

All people that on earth do dwell,
Sing to the Lord with cheerful voice:
Him serve with fear, his praise forth tell,
Come ye before him and rejoice.

Know that the Lord is God indeed;
Without our aid he did us make:
We are his folk, he doth us feed,
And for his sheep he doth us take.

O enter then his gates with praise,
Approach with joy his courts unto;
Praise, laud, and bless his name always,
For it is seemly so to do.

For why? The Lord our God is good,
His mercy is for ever sure;
His truth at all times firmly stood,
And shall from age to age endure.

READINGS

One or more of the following or other appropriate texts may be read.

The LORD said to Moses, "Say to all the congregation of the people of Israel, You shall be holy; for I the LORD your God am holy.

You shall do no injustice in judgment; you shall not be partial to the poor or defer to the great, but in righteousness shall you judge your neighbor. You shall not go up and down as a slanderer among your people, and you shall not stand forth against the life of your neighbor: I am the LORD.

You shall not hate your neighbor in your heart, but you shall reason with your neighbor, lest you thereby bear sin. You shall not take vengeance or bear any grudge against your own people, but you shall love your neighbor as yourself: I am the LORD."
—LEVITICUS 19:1–2, 15–18

You shall not wrong or oppress a stranger, for you were strangers in the land of Egypt. You shall not afflict any widow or orphan. If you do afflict them, and they cry out to me, I will surely hear their cry; and my wrath will burn.

—EXODUS 22:20–23

Say to those who are of a fearful heart,
   "Be strong, fear not!
Behold, your God
   will come with vengeance,
with the recompense of God,
   God will come and save you."
Then the eyes of the blind shall be opened,
   and the ears of the deaf unstopped;
then shall the lame leap like a hart,
   and the tongue of the dumb sing for joy.
For the waters shall break forth in the wilderness,
   and streams in the desert;
the burning sand shall become a pool,
   and the thirsty ground springs of water.

—ISAIAH 35:4–7

Hear, O Israel: the LORD our God is one LORD; and you shall love the LORD your God with all your heart, and with all your soul, and with all your might. And these words which I command you this day shall be upon your heart; and you shall teach them diligently to your children, and shall talk of them when you sit in your house, and when you walk by the way, and when you lie down, and when you rise.

—DEUTERONOMY 6:5–8

The Lord said to Moses, "Say to Aaron and his sons, Thus you shall bless the people of Israel: you shall say to them,
   The LORD bless you and keep you:
   The LORD'S face shine upon you, and be gracious to
      you:
   The LORD look upon you with favor, and give you
      peace.
   "So shall they put my name upon the people of Israel, and I will bless them."

—NUMBERS 6:22–27

Whereas it is the duty of all nations to acknowledge the providence of almighty God, to obey his will, to be grateful for his benefits, and humbly to implore his protection and favor: And whereas both Houses of Congress have, by their joint committee, requested me to recommend to the people of the United States, a day of public thanksgiving and prayer, to be observed by acknowledging with grateful hearts the many and signal favors of almighty God, especially by affording them an opportunity peaceably to establish a form of government for their safety and happiness. . . . Now therefore, I do recommend . . . that we may then all unite in rendering unto him our sincere and humble thanks for his kind care and protection of the people of this country.

   GEORGE WASHINGTON'S PROCLAMATION
   ESTABLISHING DAY OF THANKSGIVING, OCTOBER 3, 1789

A reflection may then be shared or a homily preached.

PSALM

The following or another psalm is prayed by all. The verses may be spoken in alternation: women/men, right side/left side, or Jews/Christians. One group speaks the first half of each verse, the other group the second half.

Praise God from the sky,
  Praise God from the heights;
Praise God, all you angels,
  Praise God, heaven's hosts,
Praise God, sun and moon,
  Praise God, all bright stars;
Praise God, skies above,
  And waters above the skies.
They praise their true Lord,
  Who ordered their making,
Who placed them for ever,
  In the courses they follow.
Praise the Lord from the earth,
  Ocean deeps and dragons,
Fire and hail, snow and smoke,
  Gale wind doing God's word;
All mountains and hills,
  All fruit trees and cedars,
All beasts, wild or tame,
  Creeping things and soaring birds;
All earth's kings and peoples,
  All earth's princes and rulers,
Young women and men,
  And the old with the young.
Praise the name of the Lord;
  God alone is worthy of honor.

God's might is above earth and sky;
  God's people rise up in power.
Israel's children are close to God,
  God the glory of all faithful people!
Praise the Lord! Hallelujah!
—PSALM 148

PRAYERS

Prayers may be invited from the assembly. Other prayers may be chosen from those found in this book. The following may be included.

Lord, we are always trying to be at home in the lands of our exile. On this holiday we join with others in this nation in giving thanks: not for power and not for wealth and not at all, Lord, for the armaments which we inflict upon the world and ourselves. But we thank you, Lord, for the ordinary goodness of our people, for the spirit of justice that now and again will shake this nation. We thank you for the beauty and fullness of the land and the people-mixing challenge of cities. We thank you for our work and our rest, one another, our homes. For all these and for all that we keep in our hearts, accept our Thanksgiving Day.

BENEDICTION

The Lord bless us and keep us!
May the face of the Lord shine upon us and be kind to us.
May the Lord look upon us with kindness and give us
  peace.

SOURCES OF TEXTS

The texts in scripture selections marked NAB are from The New American Bible with Revised New Testament. Copyright © 1986, Confraternity of Christian Doctrine, Washington, D.C. Used with permission. All rights reserved.

GIVE THANKS

GIVE THANKS: NAB

NOW THANK WE ALL OUR GOD: This is the first stanza of a seventeenth-century German hymn *(Nun danket alle Gott)* by Martin Rinckart. It was originally a blessing at table. The translation is by Catherine Winkworth (nineteenth century).

I AM COMMANDED: From *Who Is Man,* Abraham Heschel. Copyright © 1965, Stanford University Press. Used with permission.

REJOICE ALWAYS: NAB

AS I GIVE MYSELF: From "A Poem of Thanks" by Paulinus, circa 459. When he was 83 years old, the poet, a Roman living in Gaul, wrote a long autobiographical poem as an expression of thanksgiving to God for his entire life. These are the opening lines. *Prayer: Personal and Liturgical,* Agnes Cunningham. Reprinted with permission of Michael Glazier, Inc., Wilmington, Delaware.

THE TIME FOR RECITING: A story told of the Rabbi of Apt, Abraham Joshua Heschel. He lived in Poland and died in 1822. He is the namesake and great-grandfather of the twentieth-century Jewish theologian of the same name. A version of this story is found in *A Hasidic Anthology,* ed. Louis I. Newman (New York: Scribner and Sons, 1934; Schocken Books, 1963). An earlier Hebrew source is *Midor Dor,* ed. M. Lipson (Tel Aviv: 1929). The prayer referred to, "I offer thanks to you," is quoted in Chapter 6 as "I am grateful to you."

LET US GIVE THANKS: Two lines of the dialogue that introduce the eucharistic prayer in many ancient and modern Christian liturgies. These lines entered Christian prayer directly from contemporary Jewish prayer texts where they served a like purpose: invitation to join in a prayer of thanksgiving (at the end of a meal).

YOUR WONDROUS DEEDS

WE GIVE YOU THANKS: NAB

PRAISED ARE YOU . . . IN THE WORLD: The original blessing reads: "Praised be he who has such in his world." The source is Talmud, *Tractate Berakhot* (Blessings), p. 58b. In its form used in Jewish liturgy, it reads: "Praised are you, Lord our God, ruler of the universe, who has such beauty in his world." This blessing is traditionally recited on the occasion of seeing trees and creatures of striking beauty.

PRAISED ARE YOU . . . ALL THAT IS GOOD: This is the traditional Jewish blessing recited by one who has been spared from mishap, including recovering from serious illness, returning safely from a dangerous journey, surviving any kind of danger, and surviving childbirth. The blessing itself is recited by the individual and the congregation responds with "May . . . good." It is customary to recite this during the Torah reading part of the service. The present translation is from *Siddur Sim Shalom* (New York: The Rabbinical Assembly, 1985), p. 143. The prayer is known as *Birkhat ha-Gomeil,* the "blessing of the redeemed."

EVERY DAY: Ben Zion Bokser was an American rabbi born in Poland (1907–1984). "God's Prayer" is from his *The Gifts of Life and Love* (New York: Hebrew Publishing Company, 1958; revised edition, 1975), p. 148.

GLORY BE TO GOD: Poem by Gerard Manley Hopkins, nineteenth-century poet and Jesuit.

THERE IS A QUESTION: From *Who Is Man,* Abraham Heschel. Copyright © 1965, Stanford University Press. Used with permission.

ALL YOU WHO WORSHIP HIM: From the work of the contemporary American poet Catherine de Vinck. From *A Book of Uncommon Prayers,* copyright © 1976, Catherine de Vinck. Used with permission of Alleluia Press, Allendale, New Jersey.

TO BE A PERSON: From *Who Is Man,* Abraham Heschel. Copyright © 1965, Stanford University Press. Used with permission.

CREATION

IT IS GOOD TO GIVE THANKS: NAB

PRAISED ARE YOU . . . OF THE GROUND: The traditional Jewish blessing recited before eating food that grows in the ground. The talmudic source is *Tractate Berakhot* (Blessings), p. 35a.

WE GIVE THANKS: A blessing thanking God for rain. The talmudic source is *Tractate Berakhot* (Blessings), p. 59b.

AS CLAY WE ARE: From the Evening Service on Yom Kippur. The translation (altered) is from *High Holiday Prayer book,* compiled and arranged by Morris Silverman (Hartford: Prayer Book Press, 1951), p. 234. This is from an anonymous medieval *piyyut,* or liturgical poem, possibly of twelfth-century origin (A. Z. Idelson, *Jewish Liturgy* [New York: Holt, Rinehart and Winston, 1932], p. 237).

PRAISED ARE YOU . . . TO ENJOY: The traditional Jewish blessing recited on seeing trees in bloom in springtime. The talmudic source is *Tractate Berakhot* (Blessings), p. 43b.

MOST HIGH: Called "The Canticle of the Sun" or "The Canticle of the Creatures," this text was composed in the thirteenth century by Francis of Assisi, the "little poor man." The address of all creatures as "brother" and "sister" expressed the way of life Francis had chosen.

STEWARDSHIP

FATHER, ALL POWERFUL: Excerpt (altered) from the English translation of *The Roman Missal.* Copyright © 1973, International Committee on English in the Liturgy (ICEL). Used with permission. All rights reserved. This is one of the texts that begin the eucharistic prayer in Roman Catholic liturgy on Sundays. The eucharistic prayer is a text of praise and thanksgiving that is the center of the Mass.

EARTH'S CRAMMED WITH HEAVEN: Elizabeth Barrett Browning, nineteenth century.

WE ARE AS: From *Your Word Is Near,* Huub Oosterhuis. Copyright © 1968, Newman Press. Used with permission of Paulist Press. Oosterhuis is a contemporary Dutch poet and theologian.

BLESSED ARE YOU: A blessing of natural products, taken from the Roman Catholic *Book of Blessings.* Copyright © 1988, ICEL. Used with permission. All rights reserved.

ALMIGHTY AND: A blessing of manufactured things taken from the Roman Catholic *Book of Blessings.* Copyright © 1988, ICEL. Used with permission. All rights reserved.

WHEN THE HOLY ONE: From *Midrash Ecclesiastes Rabbah* VII:12,1 commenting on Ecclesiastes 7:13. The translation is by Byron Sherwin.

FOR THE FRUIT: A hymn text, "For the Fruits of His Creation," by the contemporary poet and composer Fred Pratt Green. Copyright © 1970, Hope Publishing Company, Carol Stream, Illinois 60188. Used with permission. All rights reserved.

GIFT OF LIGHT

THE SUN TO RULE: From *The Psalms: A New Translation* published by Wm. Collins Sons & Co., Ltd. Used with permission of A. P. Watt, Ltd., on behalf of The Grail, England.

YOU ILLUMINE: From the traditional Jewish liturgy for weekday mornings, including holy days that fall on weekdays. The translation is from *Siddur Sim Shalom,* p. 343.

PRAISED ARE YOU: From the traditional Jewish liturgy for evening prayer. It is recited on weekdays, Sabbath and holy days. The translation is from *Siddur Sim Shalom,* p. 281.

O GOD, WHO MADE THE SUN: One of the ancient texts that manifests the joining of Christian and pre-Christian expressions among the Celtic peoples. From *Prayers of the Gael,* R. MacCraigh. Published by B. Herder, St. Louis, Missouri.

O GOD, WHOSE HAND: This hymn for the fourth day of creation, part of a cycle of hymns for each day of the week, has been sung at evening prayer on Wednesdays. The author is unknown but the texts have often been attributed to Gregory the Great, bishop of Rome at the end of the sixth century. The translation is from *The Short Breviary.* Copyright © 1962, Order of St. Benedict, Inc. Used with permission of The Liturgical Press, Collegeville, Minnesota.

MY FATHER: From *The Collected Works of Joseph Hayyim Brenner,* vol. 5 (Hebrew) (Tel Aviv, 1924), p. 189. An English translation appears in Shalom Spiegel, *Hebrew Reborn* (New York: World, 1930; Philadelphia: Jewish Publications Society, 1962). The translation given here is from *Language of Faith,* ed. Nahum N. Glatzer (New York: Schocken Books, 1947), p. 59.

I GIVE THANKS TO YOU: From the "Psalms of Thanksgiving" found among the Dead Sea Scrolls. The translation is from *The Dead Sea Scriptures,* Theodore H. Gaster (New York: Doubleday, 1957), p. 142.

O KING OF GLORY: A translation from an ancient Celtic prayer. Copyright © Diarmuid O'Laoghaine.

WE SHOULD THANK: This is an introductory paragraph to the *Hallel* recited during the Passover *Seder*. The translation is from *The Passover Haggadah,* ed. Morris Silverman (Bridgeport: Prayer Book Press, 1972), p. 29.

BEGINNING THE DAY, ENTERING THE NIGHT

O LORD OUR GOD: This is from the traditional Jewish liturgy for the evening service. It is recited on weekdays, Sabbaths and holy days. The exact wording differs depending on the ritual used. While the text of the prayer is not given in the Talmud, it is referred to there in *Tractate Berakhot* (Blessings), pp. 4b, 9b.

TO YOU I PRAY: NAB

WHO WAS EVER: From *Selected Works II,* Rainer Maria Rilke, translated by J. B. Leishman. Copyright © 1960, The Hogarth Press, Ltd. Reprinted by permission of New Directions Publishing Corporation.

I AM GRATEFUL: Blessing recited by Jews upon awakening in the morning. See, e.g., *Siddur Sim Shalom,* p. 3. Since it is recited before one has a chance to wash, "God" is not mentioned.

PRAISED ARE YOU: The Talmud, in *Tractate Berakhot* (Blessings), p. 54a, requires reciting this blessing upon significant occasions, such as building a new house or buying new vessels. Today it is customary to recite this blessing upon using something new for the first time, such as wearing new clothing. It also is often recited upon the attainment of a milestone in life.

WHEN THEY SANG: From *The Penguin Book of Hebrew Verse,* ed. T. Carmi (Allen Lane, 1981). Copyright © 1981, T. Carmi. Used with permission of Penguin Books, Ltd., London.

IN THE MORNING: From *The Psalms* (an Inclusive Language Version based on the Grail Translation from the Hebrew). Copyright © 1963, 1986, Ladies of the Grail (England). Used with permission of GIA Publications, Inc., Chicago, Illinois, exclusive agent. All rights reserved.

OF THE LIGHT: From a third-century manuscript.

AS SOON AS I LIE DOWN: NAB

I GIVE THANKS: From the "Psalms of Thanksgiving" found among the Dead Sea Scrolls. The translation is from *The Dead Sea Scriptures,* Theodore H. Gaster (New York: Doubleday, 1957), p. 133.

HAVE MERCY ON ME: From an ancient Celtic prayer to be said on awakening in the night. Copyright © Diarmuid O'Laoghaine.

BODY

PRAISED ARE YOU: Traditional prayer recited by Jews after going to the bathroom. It celebrates the gift of the body. The talmudic source is *Tractate Berakhot* (Blessings), p. 60b. The translation is from *Siddur Sim Shalom,* p. 7.

WE ARE THE WORK: By the contemporary Dutch poet and theologian, Huub Oosterhuis. From *Your Word Is Near.* Copyright © 1968, Newman Press. Used with permission of Paulist Press.

WE GIVE YOU THANKS: From *Stay With Us,* Francois Chagneau. Copyright © 1971, Newman Press. Used with permission of Paulist Press.

BEFORE I WAS BORN: From *The Jewish Poets of Spain,* David Goldstein. Poem by Solomon ibn Gabriol, 11th-century Spain. Used with permission of David Higham Associates, Ltd. for the publisher, Penguin Books.

FOR EVERY BREATH: From *Midrash Genesis Rabbah* 14:9. The translation is by Byron Sherwin.

WITH OPEN EARS: Prayer in thanksgiving for the gift of hearing from *Prayers for the Domestic Church: A Handbook for Worship in the Home,* Edward M. Hays, 1979. Used with permission of Forest of Peace Books, Inc., Easton, Kansas.

WHEN ONE DRESSES: A citation from the Talmud, *Tractate Berakhot* (Blessings), p. 60b. Jews recite this blessing as part of the daily morning liturgy.

MEALS

THE EYES OF ALL: From Psalm 104.

LORD, BLESS THIS FOOD: From an ancient Celtic prayer for blessing before meals. Copyright © Diarmuid O'Laoghaine.

FROM MANY HOMES: From a prayer at table when the extended family has gathered. *Table Prayerbook.* Liturgy Training Publications, 1980.

PRAISE TO YOU: The blessing for nourishment, an initial part of the traditional Jewish grace after meals. According to the legend, it was composed by Moses in gratitude for the manna with which God sustained Israel in the desert.

PRAISED ARE YOU . . . FROM THE EARTH: Traditional Jewish blessing recited before a meal, specifically before eating bread. The talmudic source for this blessing is *Tractate Berakhot* (Blessings), p. 35a.

PRAISED ARE YOU . . . NOURISHMENT: Traditional Jewish blessing recited before eating a variety of foods—other than bread—that are prepared from grains such as wheat, barley, oats, etc. The talmudic source for this blessing is *Tractate Berakhot* (Blessings), p. 36b.

PRAISED ARE YOU . . . THE VINE: Traditional Jewish blessing recited before drinking wine. The talmudic source for this blessing is *Tractate Berakhot* (Blessings), p. 35a.

EARTHMAKER: Daily prayer at meals from *Prayers for the Domestic Church: A Handbook for Worship in the Home,* Edward M. Hays, 1979. Used with permission of Forest of Peace Books, Inc., Easton, Kansas.

THE HASIDIC MASTER: Barukh of Medziboz, died 1811, was a Polish hasidic master, and was the grandson of the Baal Shem Tov, the founder of Hasidism. The original Hebrew text is found in *Miflaot ha-tzaddikim* (Warsaw: Munk, n.d.), p. 38. The English translation is by Byron Sherwin, based on that of Newman, *Hasidic Anthology,* p. 326.

HEARING, MUSIC, SILENCE

I WILL PRAISE: From *The Psalms: A New Translation for Prayer and Worship,* translated by Gary Chamberlain. Copyright © 1984, The Upper Room, 1908 Grand Avenue, Nashville, Tennessee. Used with permission of the publisher.

WITH SAINTLY SHOUT: "At a Solemn Music," John Milton, seventeenth-century poet.

IN RECEIVING: From *Who Is Man,* Abraham Heschel. Copyright © 1965, Stanford University Press. Used with permission.

ALL YOUR WORKS: Psalms 113–118 are recited on Jewish festivals such as Passover, Pentecost, Feast of Booths, Hannukah and the New Moon. This is called the prayer of "Hallel" ("Praise"). The *Hallel* concludes with the paragraph cited. *Hallel* is recited at the Passover Seder and this translation is from *The Passover Haggadah,* ed. Morris Silverman (Bridgeport: Prayer Book Press, 1972), p. 53.

LORD, MAY THE SEEDS: Prayer for times of silence and solitude from *Prayers for the Domestic Church: A Handbook for Worship in the Home,* Edward M. Hays, 1979. Used with permission of Forest of Peace Books, Inc., Easton, Kansas.

THE PSALM: From *Tales of the Hasidim: The Early Masters,* Martin Buber (New York: Schocken Books, 1981).

ONCE, ON THE EVE: Attributed to Zusya of Anipol, died 1800, a hasidic master and brother of Elimelekh of Lizensk, who lived in Poland. The citation is from Buber, p. 246.

THROUGH SONG: From *The Oath,* Elie Wiesel. Copyright © 1973, Elie Wiesel. Reprinted by permission of Random House, Inc.

SINGING IS DISCOVERED: By the contemporary Dutch poet and theologian, Huub Oosterhuis. From *Prayers, Poems and Songs,* copyright © 1970, Herder and Herder. Used with permission of Crossroad Publishing Company.

THE MARVELS OF GOD: From the writings of Hildegard of Bingen, a twelfth-century poet and nun; she was called "the Sibyl of the Rhine" for her visions, prophecies and poems. Permission to quote from *Illuminations of Hildegard of Bingen,* text by Hildegard of Bingen, commentary by Matthew Fox, copyright

© 1985 by Bear & Company, Inc., has been granted by the publisher, Bear & Company, Santa Fe, New Mexico.

COMMUNITY

WE GIVE THANKS: NAB

ONCE THERE WAS: Adapted from the Talmud, *Tractate Ta'anit* (Fasts), p. 23a. Some think that this talmudic tale served as the basis of Washington Irving's story "Rip Van Winkle."

ALMIGHTY FATHER: Prayer for a time of thanksgiving from the Roman Catholic *Book of Blessings.* Copyright © 1988, ICEL. Used with permission. All rights reserved.

WE ARE YOUR PEOPLE: Prayer recited on *Yom Kippur,* The Day of Atonement. It is probably of medieval origin. The prayer is based upon *Midrash Song of Songs Rabbah* II:16,1. The translation is from *High Holiday Prayerbook,* ed Silverman, pp. 238–39.

FROM EGYPT: Part of the traditional morning service for Jewish Sabbath and Festivals. The translation is from *Siddur Sim Shalom,* p. 237.

JUSTICE

MY SOUL: The Magnificat or Canticle of Mary, a text from the gospel of Luke that is filled with images and verses from the Hebrew Scriptures, especially from the Psalms and the Canticle of Hannah in 1 Samuel. Translation by the English Language Liturgical Consultation, formerly the International Consultation on English Texts, 1989.

WORSHIP THE LORD: Prayer for Thanksgiving based on passages from Psalms, Isaiah and Ben Sira. The excerpt is from *Siddur Sim Shalom,* p. 819.

MAY YOU ALWAYS: Excerpt (altered) from the English translation of the Roman Catholic *Rite of Marriage.* Copyright © 1969, ICEL. Used with permission. All rights reserved

O MY GOD: From *Gates of Prayer: The New Union Prayerbook* (New York: Central Conference of American Rabbis, 1975), p. 660.

LORD GOD: By the French poet and composer, Lucien Deiss. From *Biblical Prayers,* copyright © 1976, 1981, Lucien Deiss. Used with permission of World Library Publications, Inc. All rights reserved.

REDEMPTION

YOU CHANGED MY MOURNING: NAB

PRAISE TO THE ALL-MERCIFUL and THERE ARE FOUR: Both citations are from the Talmud, *Tractate Berakhot* (Blessings), p 54b. In order of sequence in the text, "There are four" precedes "Praise to." "Praise to" was a blessing recited

58

upon Rabbi Judah's recovery from illness. It relates to a person who recovers from illness being one of the four classes of people required to give thanks.

LATE HAVE I LOVED YOU: From the works of Augustine, fifth-century African bishop, philosopher, teacher and author.

HOW THANKFUL: From *The Passover Haggadah*. The Dayenu is an ancient song that accompanies the telling of the story of redemption from slavery and the recitation of the plagues.

LET YOUR MERCY: From the traditional Jewish liturgy for the daily evening service. The translation is from *Siddur Sim Shalom*, p. 207. According to Idelsoh (*Jewish Liturgy*, p. 120), it is a post-talmudic addition to the liturgy of Babylonian origin.

MODELS FOR AN ORDER OF SERVICE

COME, BLESS: NAB

PRAISE THE LORD; COME, LET US: From *The Psalms: A New Translation for Prayer and Worship,* translated by Gary Chamberlain. Copyright © 1984, The Upper Room, Nashville, Tennessee. Used with permission.

NOW THANK WE: Music for this hymn can be found in many hymnals. The name of the tune is Nun Danket.

ALL PEOPLE: Music for this hymn can be found in many hymnals. The name of the tune is Old Hundredth.

THE LORD; YOU SHALL NOT WRONG; SAY TO THOSE; HEAR, O ISRAEL; THE LORD: From the *Revised Standard Version Bible*. Copyright © 1946, 1952, 1971 by the Division of Christian Education of the National Council of Churches of Christ in the U.S.A., as emended in the *Lectionary for the Christian People,* copyright © 1988, Pueblo Publishing Company, Inc. Used with permission. All rights reserved.

PRAISE GOD: From *The Psalms: A New Translation for Prayer and Worship,* translated by Gary Chamberlain. Copyright © 1984, The Upper Room, Nashville, Tennessee. Used with permission.

LORD, WE ARE: A prayer for Thanksgiving Day from *The Table Prayerbook,* Liturgy Training Publications, 1980.

BACK COVER

IN TIME-TO-COME: From *Midrash Pesikta d'Rav Kahana* 9:12. English translation *Pesikta de-Rab Kahana,* William Braude and Israel J. Kapstein (Philadelphia: Jewish Publication Society, 1975).